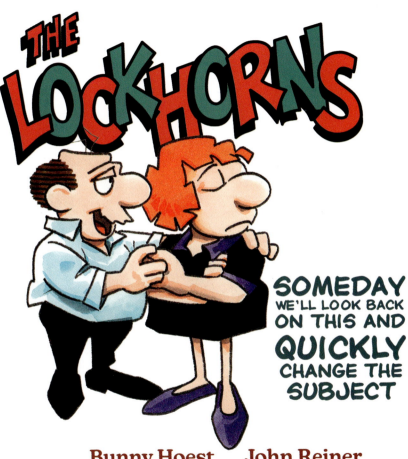

THE LOCKHORNS

SOMEDAY WE'LL LOOK BACK ON THIS AND **QUICKLY** CHANGE THE SUBJECT

Bunny Hoest   John Reiner

Andrews McMeel
PUBLISHING®

"MAYBE YOU'RE BETTER OFF COMING UP WITH
'NO RESULTS' WHEN YOU GOOGLE YOURSELF."

"ARE YOU THE OPPOSITE SEX OR AM I?"

"I KNOW WHAT HE WANTS."

"AMAZON STOCK IS DOWN SIXTEEN POINTS...
IS THE WI-FI OUT AGAIN?"

"LEROY'S THE ONLY PERSON I KNOW WHO GETS ROAD RAGE ON A STATIONARY BIKE."

"THAT'S LORETTA'S OFF-KEY LIME PIE."

"IN A WEIRD WAY, I ALMOST FEEL BAD FOR THE HACKER WHO STOLE YOUR IDENTITY."

"I'LL SHOW YOU HOW TO SAVE 100%."

"WHEN MOTHER SAYS LOOKS AND BRAINS AREN'T IMPORTANT, IT'S HER WAY OF SAYING SHE LOVES YOU."

"ACTUALLY, WE'RE CELEBRATING TWENTY YEARS OF MARRIAGE COUNSELING."

"IT'S SIRI... SHE WANTS TO KNOW WHERE WE ARE."

16

"SO . . . IS HE UP TO CODE?"

17

"THE GOOD THING ABOUT HAVING FRIENDS OUR AGE IS THAT THEY CAN'T STAY UP TOO LATE."

"THE APPLE OF MY EYE BECAME THE POTATO
OF MY COUCH."

"I CAN GO HOURS WITHOUT COFFEE...
IT'S CALLED SLEEPING."

"CAN I PROGRAM IT TO TELL LEROY NOT TO DRINK STRAIGHT OUT OF THE CARTON?"

"I NEED ONE HEAVILY LACED WITH IRONY."

"SHOULDN'T WE BE FACING IN THE SAME DIRECTION?"

"DON'T BLAME ME . . . IT'S ALL THOSE TARGETED ADS I'VE BEEN GETTING."

"THE LENHARTS SAID I COULD BRING
A MINUS ONE."

"YES, MONEY ISN'T EVERYTHING...BUT IT SURE ISN'T NOTHING, EITHER."

"THE MAIN REASON LEROY AND I STAY TOGETHER IS TO SHARE THE AMAZON PRIME ACCOUNT."

"YOU KNOW LORETTA'S MOTTO ... 'IF AT FIRST YOU DON'T SUCCEED, MAKE IT INTO A CASSEROLE.'"

"NO WONDER YOU GOT SUCH A GREAT DEAL...
THIS IS A PET HOTEL."

"CAN'T WE JUST DISAGREE TO DISAGREE?"

"THE PROBLEM WITH A SELF-PROPELLED LAWN MOWER
IS IT MOVES FASTER THAN LEROY."

"I'M RETURNING THIS GPS ... I DON'T WANT ANOTHER WOMAN'S VOICE TELLING ME WHAT TO DO."

"WELL, THIS CERTAINLY SUMS UP OUR MARRIAGE."

"DOES HE LOOK LIKE HE CAN SCAN A QR CODE?"

"IT'S NOT PROCRASTINATING IF I NEVER MEANT TO DO ANYTHING IN THE FIRST PLACE."

"MAYBE WE SHOULD RECONSIDER OUR 'NEVER GO TO BED ANGRY' RULE."

"THIS COULD BE DISASTROUS ... THEY'VE GIVEN A HURRICANE YOUR MOTHER'S NAME."

"DO YOU WANT TO BE RIGHT OR DO YOU WANT TO BE HAPPY?"

"THEY WERE ON SALE."

"YOUR LATITUDE IS CREEPING UP ON YOUR LONGITUDE."

"IS THIS THE ACTUAL MEAL OR DID YOU BURN IT IN EFFIGY?"

"I'M AFRAID I CAN'T HELP YOU, SIR...THIS COMPUTER WAS OBSOLETE BEFORE I WAS BORN."

"AND THIS IS LEROY, MY NEARLY DEPARTED."

"SO, WHEN'S YOUR WIFE COMING HOME, MR. LOCKHORN?"

"WAS THAT YOU SINGING OR A TEST OF OUR EMERGENCY BROADCAST SYSTEM?"

"THE 'I LOVE YOU'S' WOULD BE MORE MEANINGFUL WITHOUT THE CLENCHED TEETH."

"WHAT'S YOUR SECRET RECIPE, LORETTA ...
FOUR-AND-TWENTY BLACKBIRDS?"

"OUR MARRIAGE IS BASED ON TRUST AND UNDERSTANDING. LORETTA DOESN'T TRUST ME AND I DON'T UNDERSTAND HER."

"BEER IS AN ENERGY DRINK FOR LEROY... IT'S ONE OF THE FEW THINGS THAT GET HIM OFF THE COUCH."

"MARRIAGE TAKES ITS TOLL AND I NEVER HAVE THE RIGHT CHANGE."

"THANK YOU, LEROY . . . FOR GIVING ME
THE GIFT OF LAUGHTER."

"COULD YOU GIVE ME THE SILENT TREATMENT UNTIL AFTER THE GAME IS OVER?"

"THERE WERE RUMORS YOU WERE GOING
TO WEAR A SPEEDO."

"THOSE WHO FORGET THE PAST ARE CONDEMNED TO REHEAT IT."

"REMEMBER, IT'S YOUR WORD AGAINST MINE."

"THE ONLY ONES WHO LISTEN TO BOTH SIDES OF OUR ARGUMENTS ARE THE NEIGHBORS."

"MARRIAGE IS A LABOR OF LOVE . . .
IN MY CASE, HARD LABOR."

"IF TIME HEALS ALL WOUNDS, I SHOULD BE CURED BY NOW."

"YOU MUST BE LEROY . . . YOUR WIFE HAS TOLD
ME SO MUCH ABOUT YOU."

"THEY WERE ALL OUT OF VALENTINE'S DAY CARDS."

"WHEN LIFE GIVES HIM LEMONS, LEROY MAKES HARD LEMONADE."

"YES, WE'VE BEEN TOGETHER A LONG TIME, BUT YOU DON'T HAVE TO REFER TO ME AS 'OLD FAITHFUL.'"

"WHEN I SAID I WANTED SOMETHING SLINKY, LEROY, I MEANT A DRESS."

"MY WIFE IS TOO SMART FOR MY OWN GOOD."

"LEROY'S NEVER BEEN A MORNING PERSON."

"SORRY, I CAN'T GO, HERB . . . IT'S A
CATEGORY 5 ARGUMENT."

"OUR CABLE GOES OUT MORE OFTEN THAN WE DO."

"WHAT WOULD I DO WITHOUT MY WIFE?
FINISH MY OWN SENTENCES."

"I'M NOT LOOKING FOR LIFE IN THE FAST LANE, LEROY...
I'D JUST LIKE TO LEAVE THE PARKING LOT."

"I **HAD** YOUR PICTURE ON MY DESK, LORETTA, BUT THE EYES KEPT FOLLOWING ME AROUND THE ROOM."

"LEROY'S AT THE AGE WHERE HIS KNEES
BUCKLE AND HIS BELT DOESN'T."

"THEY'RE TWO SIDES OF THE SAME COIN ... THEY STAY TOGETHER, BUT CAN'T FACE EACH OTHER."

"WAKE UP, LEROY . . . IT'S TIME FOR BED."

"THERE'S NOT ENOUGH CHOCOLATE IN THE WORLD FOR LORETTA TO FORGIVE ME."

"ON THE BRIGHT SIDE, THAT PHOTO SHOULD HELP DISCOURAGE IDENTITY THEFT."

"LEG OF SALMON?"

"HEY...ISN'T THAT ONE OF YOUR FACEBOOK FRIENDS?"

"A TRAFFIC CAMERA CAUGHT YOU SPEEDING AND YOU'RE WORRIED ABOUT HOW YOUR HAIR LOOKED?"

"LEROY WANTED TO KEEP HIS BUCKET LIST SIMPLE."

"I DON'T WIN AN ARGUMENT UNTIL LORETTA SAYS 'WHATEVER.'"

"YOU WON'T BELIEVE THE DAY I'VE HAD!"

"MR. LOCKHORN, YOUR WIFE IS ON LINES ONE, TWO AND THREE."

"OF COURSE YOU CAN'T REMEMBER YOUR PIN NUMBER, LEROY. IT'S THE DATE OF OUR ANNIVERSARY."

"SOMEDAY WE'LL LOOK BACK ON THIS AND QUICKLY CHANGE THE SUBJECT."

"LEROY HAS AN ENLARGED PROCRASTINATE."

"WE'VE BEEN TOGETHER LONG ENOUGH FOR 'OUR SONG' TO ENTER THE PUBLIC DOMAIN."

"YOU'VE ACHIEVED YOUR IDEAL WEIGHT, LEROY . . . TWICE."

"'I DO' WAS PROBABLY A POOR CHOICE OF WORDS."

"SURLY TO BED, SURLY TO RISE."

"GREAT NEWS, LORETTA . . . I JUST MADE THE FINAL PAYMENT ON THE CAR."

"WHY DON'T YOU EVER KEEP THE NEW YEAR'S
RESOLUTIONS I GIVE YOU?"

"WHO PUT THE 'OUT OF ORDER' SIGN ON MY GOLF CLUBS?"

"YOU NEVER CEASE TO NOT AMAZE ME."

"LORETTA IS REALLY ANGRY AT ME."

"I'M SMARTER THAN LEROY, BUT HE'S NOT SMART ENOUGH TO KNOW IT."

"WE GET ALONG FINE WHEN WE'RE NOT FIGHTING."

"AT LEAST YOU COULD BE A COUCH **SWEET** POTATO."

"I AM SAD...LORETTA SAID SHE WOULDN'T SPEAK TO ME FOR A WEEK AND TODAY IS THE LAST DAY."

"IF YOU LEARN TO LAUGH AT YOURSELF, LEROY, YOU WON'T HAVE TIME TO DO ANYTHING ELSE."

"I'LL LISTEN, LORETTA, BUT ONLY IF IT'S A CLOSING STATEMENT."

"I'M LOOKING AT YOUR FACEBOOK PAGE... I DON'T RECALL YOUR MOUNTAIN-CLIMBING AND DIRECTING MOVIES."

"I KNOW MARRIAGE IS A UNION OF TWO SOULS...
IT'S THE UNION DUES THAT ARE KILLING ME."

"IF YOU EARNED GOOD MONEY, LEROY,
I COULDN'T WRITE BAD CHECKS."

"DOES YOUR MOTHER REALLY HAVE TO SEND YOU A SYMPATHY CARD ON OUR ANNIVERSARY?"

"WE'RE NOT LATE UNTIL WE GET THERE."

"LORETTA GOT SO ANGRY SHE SPRAINED HER THUMB TEXTING ME."

"THE WARRANTY IS GOOD FOR TWO YEARS, SO YOU SHOULD HAVE PLENTY OF TIME TO PUT IT TOGETHER."

"I LIKE TO CELEBRATE LIFE'S LITTLE VICTORIES."

"MOTHER GOT YOU A HAT FOR YOUR BIRTHDAY."

"THE CHEESE SHOULD BE FINELY AGED BY THE TIME YOU'RE READY."

"DID THE DOCTOR SPECIFY WHICH PART OF THE HORSE YOU'RE AS HEALTHY AS?"

"SORRY... I ALWAYS GET D-DAY AND OUR
ANNIVERSARY MIXED UP."

"WHAT A COINCIDENCE! MY HUSBAND WAS A RESCUE, TOO."

"WHAT WOULD YOU RECOMMEND TO NOT GET INVITED BACK?"

"LEROY'S USING HIS SMARTPHONE TO MAKE
ANOTHER DUMB PURCHASE."

"LORETTA HAS A TERRIBLE MEMORY ...
SHE REMEMBERS EVERYTHING."

"SORRY, LEROY... I DIDN'T SEE THAT SPEED BUMP!"

"I'M NOT HARD OF HEARING ... I'M **TIRED** OF HEARING."

"TEN MORE MINUTES...OR YOU COULD JUST
APOLOGIZE TO MOTHER."

"IF YOU EVER WANT TO LOSE AN ARGUMENT
WITH A WOMAN, START ONE."

"IT APPEARS YOUR WAIST IS KEEPING UP
WITH YOUR AGE."

"JUST HOW LONG HAVE YOU BEEN WITH US, LOCKHORN?"

"I THOUGHT LEROY AND I WOULD GROW OLD
TOGETHER, BUT HE BEAT ME TO IT."

"DON'T CRITICIZE MY CHOICES, LORETTA . . .
YOU WERE ONE OF THEM."

"HERE I AM TOSSING THREE COINS IN THE FOUNTAIN. AND THERE'S LEROY DIVING IN AFTER THEM."

"THANKS FOR THE 'I-TOLD-YOU-SO' CARD."

"OF COURSE I LOVE THE SIMPLE THINGS IN LIFE, LEROY ...
THAT'S WHY I MARRIED YOU."

"NOT NOW, LORETTA...JUST SEND ME AN EMOJI ABOUT HOW YOUR DAY WAS."

"I'VE DECIDED... INSTEAD OF GIVING UP THE FOODS
I LOVE, I'M GOING TO GIVE UP MIRRORS."

"WHEN YOU MAKE SOMETHING THAT'S SLOW-COOKED,
LORETTA, YOU'RE JUST DELAYING THE INEDIBLE."

"I CAN'T SLEEP, LEROY...WHY DON'T YOU
TELL ME ABOUT YOUR DAY NOW."

"THE ONES WITH THE TORCHES ARE FROM LORETTA'S FAMILY."

"LEROY PLANS SUPER BOWL SUNDAYS
TWO TO THREE YEARS AHEAD."

"I WISH THE ROAD TO RUIN HAD A LOWER SPEED LIMIT."

"LEROY'S FOUR MAJOR FOOD GROUPS ARE
ALCOHOL, CAFFEINE, SUGAR AND GREASE."

"WANTING TO WIN ARGUMENTS WITH EACH OTHER
IS WHAT'S REALLY HOLDING US TOGETHER."

"AND THAT'S ME IN THE CAST AFTER OUR FIRST DANCE TOGETHER."

"ALEXA WAS ALWAYS TAKING MY WIFE'S SIDE."

"YOU NEED TO START THINKING OUTSIDE THE BOX OF DONUTS."

"I WANTED TO LIVE HAPPILY EVER AFTER, BUT I DECIDED TO GET MARRIED INSTEAD."

"DO YOU KNOW THE DIFFERENCE BETWEEN 'SARTORIAL' AND 'SATIRICAL'?"

"I APOLOGIZE FOR NOT KNOWING WHY
I SHOULD APOLOGIZE."

"THE MOST DIFFICULT YEAR IN A MARRIAGE IS THE CURRENT ONE."

"I SEE WE'RE DINING AL FIASCO."

"LEROY'S NOT THAT INFORMED... HE THOUGHT THE MANHATTAN PROJECT WAS ABOUT IMPROVING THE COCKTAIL."

"IS THERE ANYTHING I CAN DO TO HELP
WITHOUT GETTING UP FROM THE SOFA?"

"THE NICE THING ABOUT ALWAYS BEING THE SCAPEGOAT IS IT MAKES YOU HARD TO REPLACE."

"IT WORKS . . . THE BOSS HASN'T BOTHERED ME IN A WEEK."

"WE'VE BEEN MARRIED FOR YEARS, SO WHY DO THESE TARGETED ADS KNOW ME BETTER THAN YOU DO?"

A Q&A with Bunny Hoest

creator of *The Lockhorns*

SO, BUNNY, HOW DID YOU BECOME KNOWN AS "THE CARTOON LADY"?

I didn't coin the phrase "The Cartoon Lady." It was given to me in an interview—the interviewer said he was calling me The Cartoon Lady, and the label stuck. When I began in 1973, there was only one other woman I knew who was producing a popular syndicated story strip. Dale Messick was doing *Brenda Starr*. Another friend, Selby Kelly, was assisting her husband Walt Kelly on *Pogo*. Later on, I was joined by my friends Cathy Guisewite and Lynn Johnston, and now I am happy to say that there are more women creators in our ranks.

Working with Bill (Bill Hoest, Bunny's husband and creator of *The Lockhorns*), we developed two more syndicated features (*Agatha Crumm* and *What a Guy!*), and three weekly panels (*Howard Huge*, based on our family dog, *Laugh Parade*, a column in *Parade Magazine*, and *Bumper Snickers*, a weekly panel in *The National Enquirer*). And I've been at it since then, with original artwork (no reruns!) every day for over fifty years (that's over 30,000 for *The Lockhorns* alone).

My biggest challenge was when I lost Bill. I had to decide whether I wanted to go on at all. At the recommendation of a friend and colleague, Mort Drucker of *Mad Magazine*, John Reiner joined us as Bill's assistant when Bill was diagnosed with terminal cancer. I asked John whether he thought we could continue, and John said he would try. So, I said, "Let's give it a shot!" The irony is that I've now been producing *The Lockhorns* longer with John than with Bill.

WHERE DO YOU GET THE IDEAS FOR THE COMICS?

I get ideas from observing people around me, from readers, from you! I watch what people are doing and how they interact with one another. I take copious notes about how funny people are. It's a "reality" strip! It's not at all autobiographical. Bill and I had a wonderful marriage. I started life as a high school English teacher and use what I taught then for our comics. The essence of humor is often gross exaggeration of a real situation and even hyperbole or subtle understatement. I'm still using this technique . . . I take a real situation, for example, and exaggerate it to show the absurdity of people having biting conversations with their partners, their best friends. *The Lockhorns* is my plea for people to be kind to one another and not to demean their mate. We use humor as a tool to make this point.

YOU'VE BEEN WORKING WITH JOHN REINER SINCE 1986. WHAT IS YOUR PROCESS FOR COLLABORATION?

In our cartoons, we start with the caption. I supply the gag line, and John draws all of the wonderful artwork that goes with it. I treat *The Lockhorns* as a stage set and the characters enter to deliver their lines. Once we have the caption, John does a pencil sketch first, and I look at the sketch and sometimes adjust the caption. Then, John prepares the finish. John still does his beautiful artwork entirely by hand. He is incredibly talented, as demonstrated in everything we produce.

LEROY AND LORETTA OFTEN DIRECT HILARIOUS, BUT POINTED, BARBS AT ONE ANOTHER, AND YET THERE'S STILL A WARMTH, AFFECTION, AND LOYALTY BETWEEN THEM. AS THE WRITER OF *THE LOCKHORNS*, HOW DO YOU MAINTAIN THE BALANCE IN THEIR RELATIONSHIP? WHY DO THEY STAY TOGETHER?

We are careful to give Loretta and Leroy equal time. To reassure people that Loretta and Leroy love each other and are committed to one another always, we also insert what we call "Loving Lockhorns" to offset the banter.

From reader feedback, we seem to hit the nail on the head. We hear that the banter and one-liners are a reflection of many couples who live together and get under one another's skin from time to time. We are thrilled that they see how humor can help relieve the frustrations and tensions that can pile up through the daily stresses of life. The panels make a stressful situation something to laugh at.

THE LOCKHORNS WAS ONE OF THE MOST WIDELY READ COMIC STRIPS OF THE TWENTIETH CENTURY AND REMAINS SO TODAY. WHAT KIND OF THINGS HAVE YOU HEARD FROM READERS OVER THE YEARS?

The feedback from readers is so gratifying. I hear from all over the world that the kinds of situations facing Loretta and Leroy are universal, timeless, and relatable to most couples in a committed relationship.

People write to us and say that they burst out laughing when a situation has arisen similar to those confronting Loretta and Leroy. Marriage counsellors and self-help groups contact us and say that their clients and members frequently bring in our comic panels and that the humor relieves tension between them and their loved ones.

We have frequently gotten fan mail from people saying, "You must have been looking in our window." Or, "You've been hiding in my closet. I just said that to my partner (or wish I had!)." One reader wrote to thank us for a panel involving Loretta having a fender-bender on the day that the reader had a fender-bender herself and how it had made her laugh out loud. It's gratifying and humbling that we can have a real effect on people's lives . . . for the better.

HOW DO YOU KEEP THE COMIC FEELING SO FRESH AND CONTEMPORARY?

In addition to observation, we accept gags from professional writers, amateurs, family, and friends. We say that they either send in a "gem" or a "germ" of an idea. If it's a gem, we typically trim down the caption and edit it to fit the setting or situation. If it's a germ of an idea, we may overhaul it to have a tight caption and adjust the proposed setting or situation. We keep the captions short and snappy—clear and easy to read—and focused on Loretta and Leroy. Our audience is intelligent and we don't "dumb down" our humor.

The essence of the panel is the relationship between Loretta and Leroy, and yet we try to keep the feature relevant for all types of couples and situations. And naturally, we have introduced new settings along with the changing times: smartphones, electric cars, computers, by way of example. It's fresh and contemporary because we observe the changing world around us as well as receiving input from writers, family, and friends.

WHAT HAVE BEEN SOME OF THE HIGHLIGHTS OF YOUR CAREER?

We have been nominated and received awards for our work from the National Cartoonists Society. This recognition from our fellow creators is incredibly flattering. However, the most meaningful highlights are the feedback and personal stories we hear from our readers. One particular story from a few years ago stands out, and it has stayed with me.

A woman wrote in and shared that her husband had been in a serious accident, and was in a wheelchair and depressed; he wouldn't go out and was in a funk. He apparently heard that there was a new *Lockhorns* book and asked his wife to take him to the bookstore to buy it. She wrote to thank us for having brought back her husband's joy and his willingness to live. This was a particularly poignant story, but we love hearing stories from all of our readers. We love making a positive difference in people's lives.

**AFTER ALL THOSE HUNDREDS OF
VISITS TO COUPLES THERAPY, AND
FIFTY-SIX YEARS OF MARRIAGE,
DO LORETTA AND LEROY HAVE ANY
ADVICE FOR COUPLES OUT THERE?**

Be kind to one another! I try to show the absurdity of demeaning one's partner, one's best friend. Keep your sense of humor! A sense of humor is the best way to deal with the stresses of daily life. And keep smiling!

Pam Setchell, Viewpoint Photography

Andrews McMeel Publishing
a division of Andrews McMeel Universal
1130 Walnut Street, Kansas City, Missouri 64106

www.andrewsmcmeel.com

25 26 27 28 29 IGO 10 9 8 7 6 5 4 3 2 1

ISBN: 978-1-5248-9876-2

Library of Congress Control Number: 2024949409

Editor: Lucas Wetzel
Art Director: Brittany Lee
Production Editor: Dave Shaw
Production Manager: Chadd Keim

ATTENTION: SCHOOLS AND BUSINESSES

Andrews McMeel books are available at quantity discounts with bulk purchase for educational,
business, or sales promotional use. For information, please e-mail the Andrews McMeel Publishing
Special Sales Department: sales@andrewsmcmeel.com.